EXPERIMENTS WITH ELECTRICITY

Written by
Mignonne Gunasekara

My First EXPERIMENTS

KidHaven PUBLISHING

Published in 2022 by
KidHaven Publishing, an Imprint of Greenhaven Publishing, LLC
29 East 21st Street
New York, NY 10010

This edition is published by arrangement with Booklife Publishing

Edited by: John Wood
Designed by: Brandon Mattless

Cataloging-in-Publication Data

Names: Gunasekara, Mignonne.
Title: Experiments with electricity / Mignonne Gunasekara.
Description: New York : KidHaven Publishing, 2022. | Series: My first experiments | Includes glossary and index.
Identifiers: ISBN 9781534538689 (pbk.) | ISBN 9781534538702 (library bound) | ISBN 9781534538696 (6 pack) | ISBN 9781534538719 (ebook)
Subjects: LCSH: Electricity--Experiments--Juvenile literature. | Electricity--Juvenile literature.
Classification: LCC QC527.2 G858 2022 | DDC 537.078--dc23

Printed in the United States of America

CPSIA compliance information: Batch #CSKH22: For further information contact Greenhaven Publishing LLC, New York, New York at 1-844-317-7404.

Please visit our website, www.greenhavenpublishing.com. For a free color catalog of all our high-quality books, call toll free 1-844-317-7404 or fax 1-844-317-7405.

PHOTO CREDITS

Images are courtesy of Shutterstock.com. With thanks to Getty Images, Thinkstock Photo, and iStockphoto.

Cover – babayuka, Africa. Recurring Images (cover and internals) – ilkayalptekin (background pattern), The_Pixel (grid), balabolk (headers and vectors), wildfloweret (boxes), Steve Paint (arrows), yana shypova (speech bubbles), Tsaranna (vector frames and boxes).

p4-5 – Pormezz, S.Z., a Sk, paulaphoto, Mike McDonald p6-7 – Iakov Filimonov, kwanchai.c p8-9 – 2p2play, ANGHI, Monkey Business Images, Smileus p10-11 – Costazzurra, JEONGHYEON NOH, ristesi goce, Rudmer Zwerver p12-13 – Flegere, Kang Sunghee, TADDEUS p14-15 – Photo smile, yusufdemirci p18-19 – AlokVerma, Anton Prohorov, Bilanol, EHStockphoto, Lakeview Images, matsabe, Rad K, NetPhotographer, ThamKC p22-23 – Rawpixel.com

CONTENTS

Words that look like <u>this</u> can be found in the glossary on page 24.

Hello, SCIENTISTS!

Science is about learning why and how everything works. A scientist's job is to find the answers to those questions.

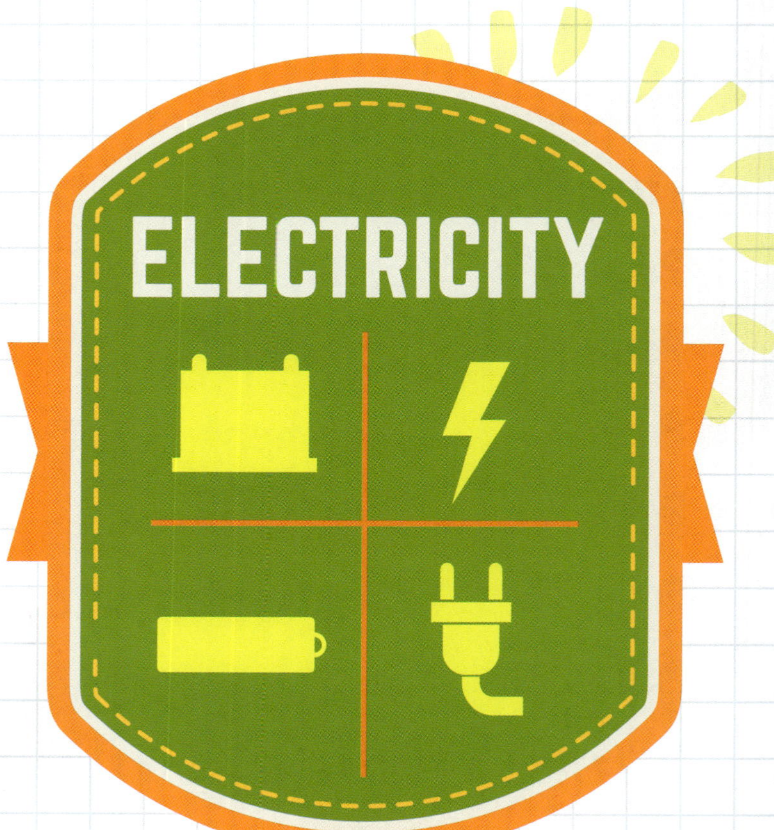

Today, we are going to learn about electricity. We will also be doing some fun experiments to help us learn.

If you complete them, you will earn your Electricity Badge!

Let's get that badge!

What Is ELECTRICITY?

Electricity is used to give power to electronic devices. We use electricity a lot in our everyday lives, to work and to play.

Here are some examples of devices that use electricity. How many of them have you come across?

Speakers

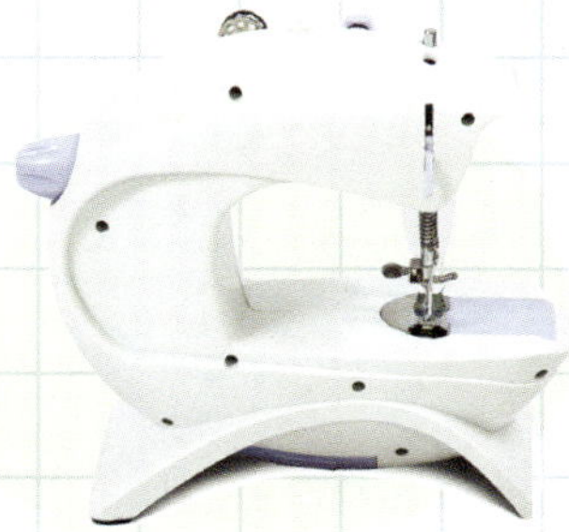

Sewing machine

Kettle

Mixer

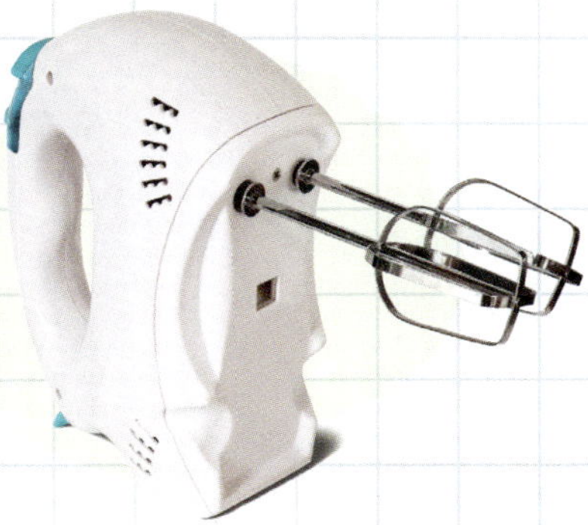

Computer

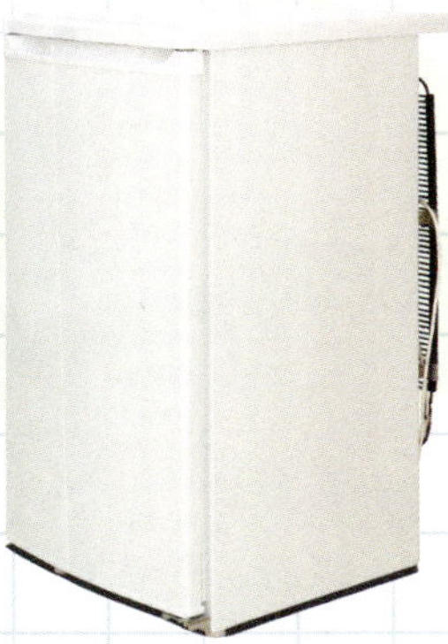

Fridge

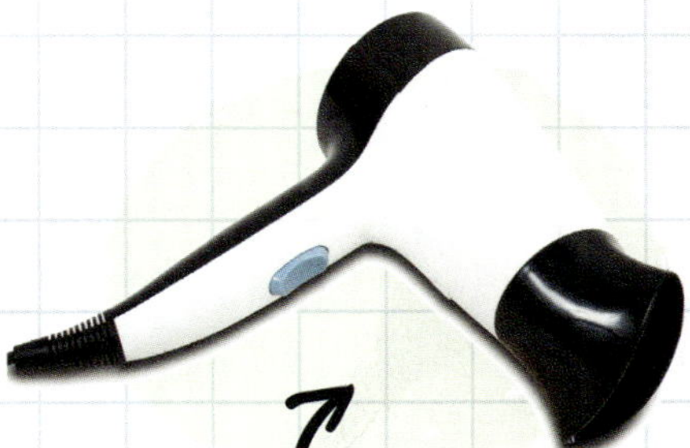

Hair dryer

Vacuum cleaner

How to Use ELECTRICITY

Most electrical devices need to be plugged into a socket before they can work. Then you may need to turn a switch on. Now the electricity is flowing and can power your device.

The electricity that comes out of a socket is household electricity.

Batteries can be used to power electronic devices so that they don't need to be plugged in. This is useful because you can carry the device around with you.

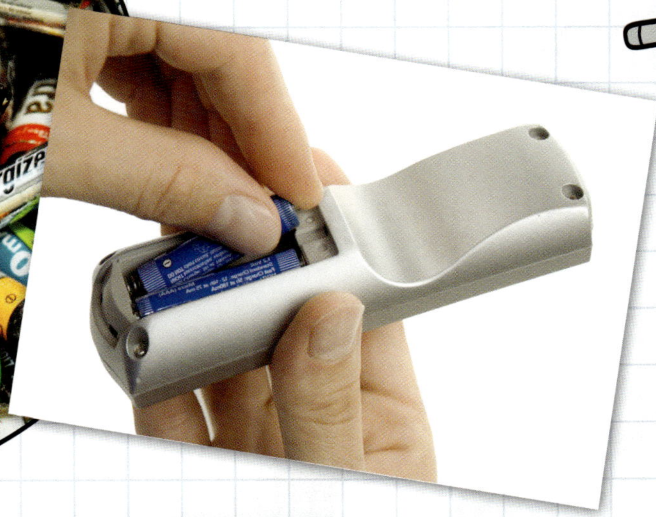

Some batteries can only be used once before they run out of power forever. Many devices have <u>rechargeable</u> batteries. These can be used again and again.

POWER UP

A lot of electricity is generated by power plants. These power plants burn fossil fuels to generate electricity. Electricity generated from fossil fuels is bad for our planet because it makes climate change worse.

A coal power plant

There are some ways of generating electricity that do not harm the planet or make climate change worse. These are called renewable sources of electricity.

Wind turbine

Hydroelectric power plant

Solar panels

Renewable sources include solar power, wind power, and hydropower.

It is important not to waste electricity. Always switch off electrical devices when you are not using them.

Conductors & INSULATORS

Conductors are things that allow electricity to pass through them. Metals are very good electrical conductors. Copper is one of the best metal conductors, so it is often used to make wires.

Copper wire

Insulators are things that do not conduct electricity because electricity cannot flow through them. Plastic, glass, wood, and rubber are all insulators. Insulators can block electricity from flowing where it is not wanted.

That's why wires are wrapped in rubber – to keep you from getting an electric shock when you touch them!

CIRCUITS

Circuits are made up of <u>components</u>, joined by wires. Circuits are powered by a power source such as a battery. Electricity can only move through a circuit if it is in a complete loop.

This is how electricity flows through a circuit.

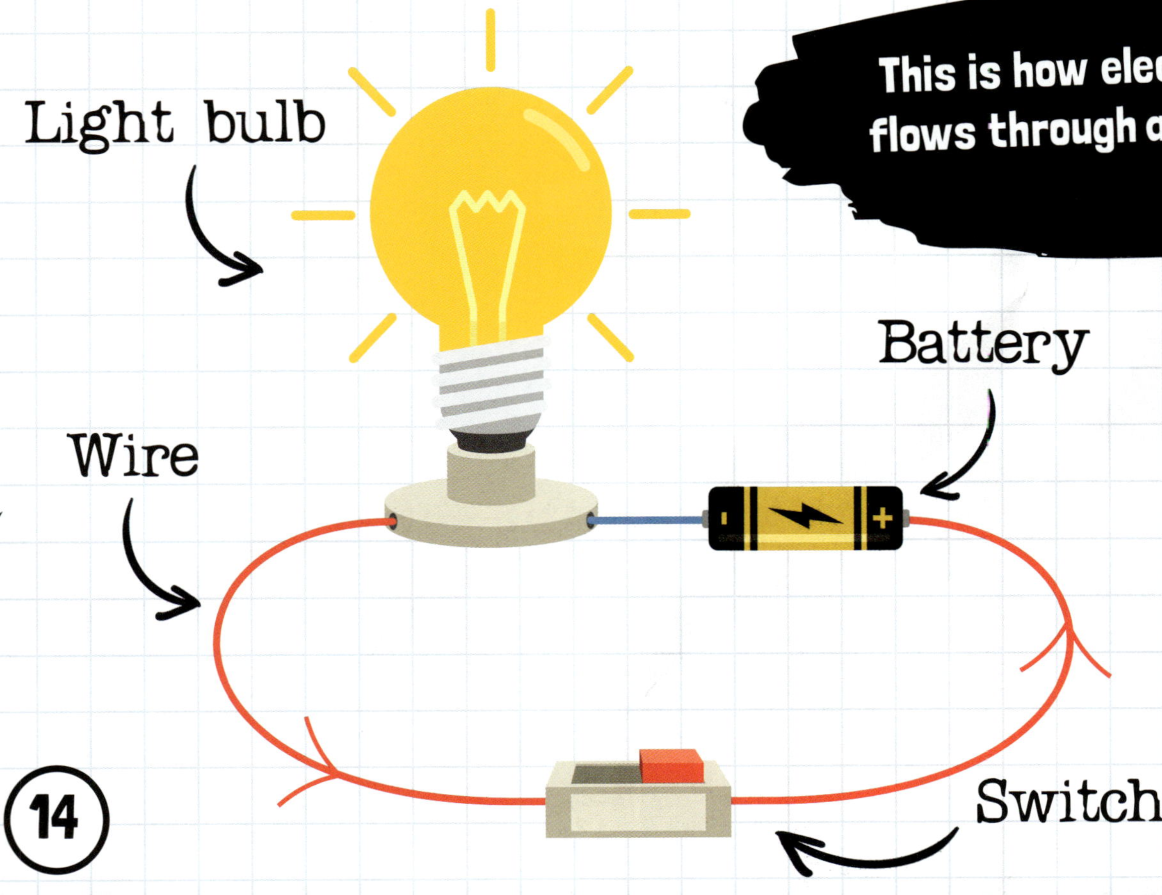

A switch can turn a circuit on by completing the loop, or off by breaking the loop. When the circuit is complete, any components it has will be powered.

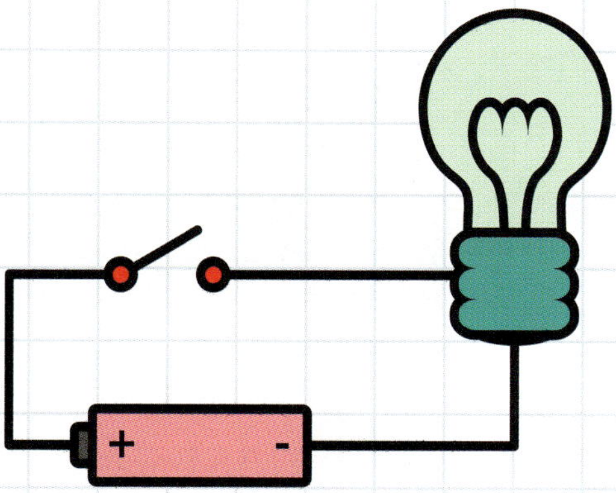

Switch off

Switch on

When a circuit is broken, electricity does not flow. This means the components will not be powered.

Experiment: What CONDUCTS?

Which materials from around your home are conductors, and which are insulators? Try to find as many different materials as you can, and we'll test them to see if they conduct electricity or not.

Ask an adult to help you.

You will need:
- Two AA batteries
- A small bulb
- Aluminium foil, rolled into a wire
- Objects to test from around the house

1) Put the positive (+) end of one battery against the negative (-) end of another.

2) Use the foil wire to connect your batteries to the bottom of the metal part of the bulb.

3) Complete the circuit by touching an object to the other end of the batteries and the metal part of the bulb.

4) If the bulb lights up, the object is a conductor. If not, it is an insulator.

Danger, DANGER

It is important to be careful around electricity, as it can be very dangerous. Follow these steps to stay safe.

Never poke your fingers or other objects into sockets.

Never use electrical devices around water, or with wet hands.

Never pull a plug out of its socket by its cord – hold it at the plug.

Do not plug lots of devices into one socket.

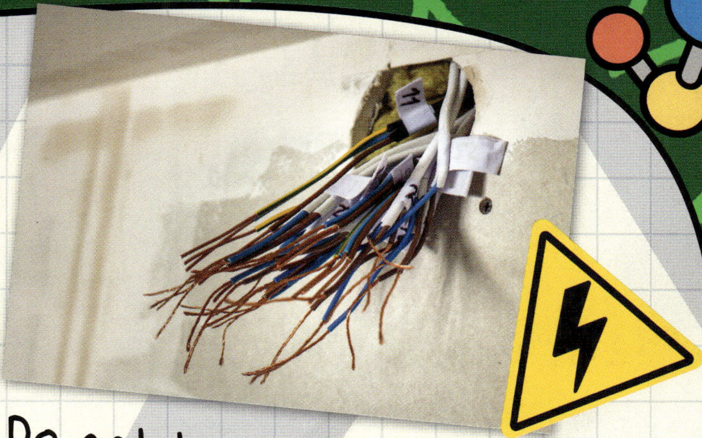

Do not touch any wires with the metal part showing.

Do not go onto electrified railroad tracks.

Do not go near pylons or substations.

Substation

Look out for these signs. They will warn you about danger.

Experiment: Magic STATIC

Static electricity is a kind of electricity that stays on the surface of insulators. Let's see it in action!

You will need:
- An inflated balloon
- Your hair
- A tap with running water
- An empty aluminium can

1) Rub the balloon against your dry hair.

2) Gently move the balloon away from your head. Is your hair standing on end? That's because of static electricity.

3) Turn on the tap so there is a gentle flow of water.

4) Rub the balloon on your hair again, and hold it near the stream of water. Static electricity should make the water bend.

5) Lay the aluminium can on a table so it can roll.

6) Rub the balloon on your hair again, then hold it near the can. Does the can roll toward the balloon? That's static, back at it!

The Badge CEREMONY

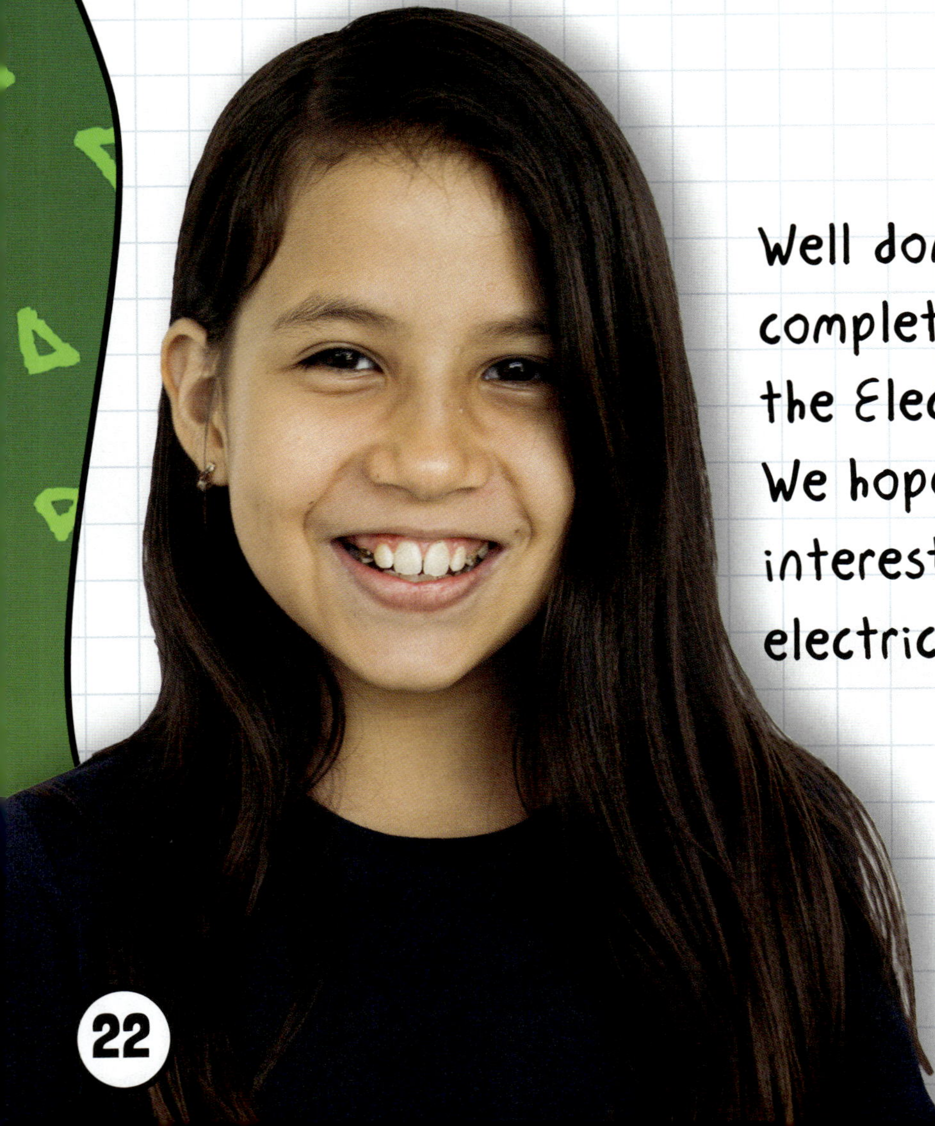

Well done! Now that you have completed the experiments, the Electricity Badge is yours. We hope you learned some interesting things about electricity!

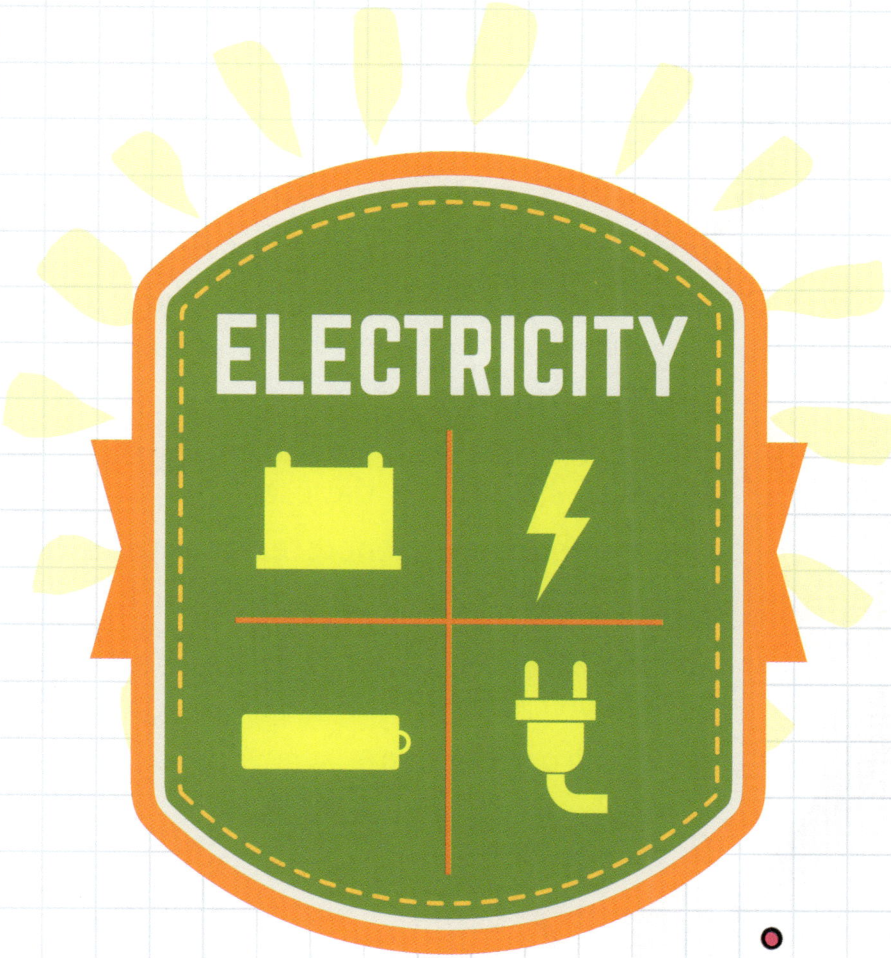
ELECTRICITY

GLOSSARY

climate change	a change in the typical weather of a large area
components	(in a circuit) devices, such as bulbs and switches, that are connected by wires
devices	machines or inventions made to do something
experiments	tests done to explore and try new things
fossil fuels	fuels such as coal, oil, and gas that formed millions of years ago from the remains of animals and plants
generated	created, produced, or made
household electricity	the general-purpose power supply that is often supplied directly to the user
hydroelectric	related to energy generated using the flow of water
inflated	made larger using air
rechargeable	able to have its electrical energy restored by connection to a power supply
solar power	energy from the sun
surface	the outside layer of something

INDEX